For Pomegranates

PARDIS ALIAKBARKHANI

For Pomegranates
Copyright © 2021 by Pardis Aliakbarkhani

All rights reserved. No part of this publication may be reproduced, distributed, or transmitted in any form or by any means, including photocopying, recording, or other electronic or mechanical methods, without the prior written permission of the author, except in the case of brief quotations embodied in critical reviews and certain other non-commercial uses permitted by copyright law.

Tellwell Talent
www.tellwell.ca

ISBN
978-0-2288-4962-9 (Hardcover)
978-0-2288-4963-6 (Paperback)

For my sister, my sisters, my mother, and all mothers.

Preface

For Pomegranates
Women with leather on their backs
From carrying their family's hopes on their shoulders
Women with sweetness in their hearts
From seeing the world as a single lover
Women that are hard to crack into
With intricate worlds buried within them
Women who feed generations with
Their wisdom and sacrifice

I am clapping for you, sister
Even when my clap is a smile
Even when my clap is a nod
Even when my clap is silence
I am praising you, rooting for you
Praying to God for your abundance
Even when the clap falters and disappears into a smile
Shrinks into a nod
Or acknowledges itself quietly in the silence
I am here for you loudly and in all ways

I am mother to my mother and my sisters and myself
I am mother to my dreams and my failures and my own health
I am a mother before passion swells my belly with new life
I am a mother the moment I act in the spirit of love
Cradling innocence and wonder in myself

I pray that I do not bury my sadness in my children
I do not want them to inherit my tears
But some pain lingers through generations
Is distilled in the water of a mother's womb
My own mother's cries still echo in my chest
I am still answering for them, dissecting my trauma from hers
Hoping to heal them both somehow

You think you are a storm
Because you speak in rain on cloudy days
But I know that within you
Kindness radiates with all the warmth
Of the sun
That your eyes sparkle with goodness, stars to map home
And your lips curve into rainbows
With the sincerity of your smile
You are not a storm alone
You are the beauty of the entire sky

I walk down the street
A rattle in my bones
Eyes that are staring me down like knives
Poised against my throat
I cringe with every step
Every bump on the road
Sends shivers down my body
The skin there, you know
Is this too revealing for the daytime?
Did I over curl my hair?
Did my lipstick spill onto my teeth?
Did I overstate my derriere?
So many thoughts buzzing
In the honeycomb of my mind
Before I straighten myself and think,
"Let them kiss my behind!"

Your body is a home, a temple, a lover, a friend
In pain, can become a fleshy prison, an enemy
To be loving is to be kind to everyone
Not knowing who, or what they are living with

Burying yourself in busyness
Can bury the pain, too, for a time
But eventually the work will be done
Life will demand pause
And you will be forced to sit in the pit you dug
To hide away from your sadness
With all the things you are afraid to be sad about
So, feel it, even if it hurts
Even if you are afraid now
Feel it so it doesn't make a crater out of you later

Allow the woman you are
To exist without apology
Then manifest her loudly

A seed doesn't know it will someday become a mighty oak
A sapling might even doubt this
But their roots know
The soil knows
People are this way, too

Failure is a road to the road to success
Every time I fall
I straighten my back
I stand tall
Ready to fight back
Failure is a road to the road to success
Every time I am humbled
I learn to adapt
I have fallen, I have tumbled
I have scraped my knees pleading
I am a monument of my failures
A pillar of my bleeding
But failure is a road to the road to success
And if I am still going, I am still growing
Closer still, to the road to success

In my solitude
I recover parts of myself that are lost in the noise
I am not lonely in my alone
I am resurrecting the woman I am
The woman I was
Manifesting from their combined wisdom
The woman I need to become

We can lose memories to trauma
Years, even
Can dissolve when the lightning strikes hard enough
How easy it becomes then to mistake abuse as tradition
When little else remains to compare
But I wield the crackle of thunder in my throat
And when I speak
I reclaim the power of the storm
Without becoming engulfed in it
Power is my tradition
Mercy is my tradition
Love is my tradition
Justice is my tradition
Healing is my tradition

The body carries wars
In its bones, in its aches
It is the healing of the mind that can dissolve many a malady
You say, "A back is a back,"
Weighed down by tissue, and not tears
Never the burden of too many tragedies
Warping an unsuspecting spine, lumbering a steady gait
But a hand is a hand, connected still
To its roots, like a flower's stem
That slumps when it feeds on more shrapnel than soil

Crawl into your bed in comfort
Leave your mind to rest on your pillow
Tomorrow's worries do not belong here
Sink into sleep, suspended from reality
Dreams carrying you into realms of ecstasy
Splitting from your body to the belonging of the night
Before you are made anew in the morning light

Silence is softening

Grief lives in smiles, in tears, in anger
Grief is the vine that grows along the windows
Outside the house that Joy has built
Never consuming it, but decorating it with warped reminders
Grief says,
"My greens are here and you will never be rid of me."
To which Joy replies, "You are here. But this is still my home. I can still see the sun. I can still open the windows and taste the breeze. *You are here but you are not everything.*"

Honey will remember the shape of the honeycomb
Long after it leaves the hive
It is imprinted somewhere deep in its consciousness
A place that transcends the physical world of bees
And their labour
Of flowers and their pollen
Bears, man, and their honey lust
Honey remembers the honeycomb
Even when it is torn from its home
Alienated from its nature
Bottled golden molasses
Trauma stings
Imprints its face through generations this way

You can't shake their words
I understand that they echo in your ears
Their poignant jabs, eliciting all your deepest fears
When will you outgrow them?
When will the bells stop ringing?
When will the stillness that calms you, reign again?
You will find the quiet
When you pull out every bit of shame to the surface
And call it by its name
So what if we are ugly? Is that the worst thing a person can be?
Is ugly the greatest sin? And not malice, envy, or greed?
Speak to your fears head-on
Make them look you in the eye
If my ugly is not unhuman, why should it make me cry?
So what if I have a wonky nose and two button-like eyes?
Is my heart not still golden? Are my hands ungiving or unkind?
Then let us be ugly
As long as the soul survives
Their words are mere reminders
Of where real beauty resides

Death isn't always tragic
Sometimes it's beautiful too
A beginning from an ending
The way we fold into the earth as dirt
A casket becoming a second womb
In time our bodies feed the soil
And we are born again as a flower's bloom
Only for a winter to kiss our withered chins and say,
"You will resurrect again soon."

I am worth more than tradition
If the tradition means to diminish me
I will bind myself to new rituals I create
When I lament on my ancestors' wisdom, meditate
I will remember the rhythm of heavy beating drums
A choir of chants, of deep resounding hums
I will curate the new with the old
To survive myself and my culture
As the prophecies have foretold
I am both fire and my mother's daughter
As much as I am my own woman
And stand on my own two feet
I walk with my country's heart in my hand
Its surviving hope and born legacy

My grandmother braided her long hair with time and olive oil
Past her shoulders, past her breasts
Tickling the floor beneath her, tracing the soil
Roots reaching for roots

On the darkest night of the year
When daevas prowl, collecting fear
My people light candles and hold their loved ones near
Read from poets of old, smiling ear to ear
They celebrate the harvest
Sweeten their tea with bites of fresh fruit
Pomegranates and melons
Grapes, figs, and dates too
The lights may go out and the sun may retire
But our hearts are ever kindling
In the spirit of our fire

I lie in the grass and look up at the sky
I lose myself in the clouds
Those blushes of white
Shapes start to form—a bird, a wolf, a crescent moon
I lie there until the sun dances down to the horizon
And bleeds an orange hue
For a moment then, one that seems to last
I am content to be
A mere blade of grass
Waving with the wind
No different than the rest
No wiser to the fleeting sun
As it descends upon the West
How small we are, I think
In a universe so vast
It's all so overwhelming
Until you spend a day as grass

You are more than skin
And the mistakes your parents made

We cannot understand
As a single thread of man
Where our lives align in the greater design
Of the tapestry of men
Our purpose is far greater
Than what in life, we can plainly see
We grapple with understanding the value
Of just being you or me
Still, I promise you
Even when you are touched with doubt
You are a thread the world could not do without
Strangers that have passed you
Still remember you for your smile
When their day was empty of hope
Your kindness made it worthwhile
Friends who you've now forgotten
Live by lessons you once taught
So many beautiful ripples exist for the impact
That your very being has caused

Be kind to the thorns that grew out of you
To protect you
When you were being plucked up
By the wrong things

My mother wrote poems as a young girl
Her first of many, romancing a winter delight
She wrote about barren trees
Being tickled by a snow, pearl-white
She tells her teacher that she loves the branches
Decorated like a blushing bride
Snowflakes collecting at their feet
Like a showering of celebratory rice
But as spring arrives and the snow dissolves
The brides lose their veils
Grow green and tall
By summertime their fruit is full
And ready for its birth
Sweetening the air with their children
Trees are the first mothers on earth

My father calls me and my sister lion-women
Because no one need teach us
How to roar

When our heart has been broken
We learn to approach love with fear, not joy
Searching for evidence of more brokenness
From which we can recoil
Maybe the goal is not to fade the fear altogether
But to walk alongside it
Besides, when the fear is big enough
It's impossible to hide it
So we can approach love again
With a mingling of these two
Until the joy outweighs the fear
And tells us, "I am ready for something new."

The Luna moth
Lives not a fortnight's time
With a tiny white belly, wings a muted lime
So delicate is its existence
That often it is rarely seen
Until its body falls to decay
Crumpled beneath a hickory tree
For its short time, it propels itself to flight
Cutting through the air in search of love
Guided in the darkness by the moonlight
I have the Luna's wings imprinted in my mind
To remember, in my own way, that love is the purpose of life

Sit with your shadows
Immerse in your night
The work can't be done
By pushing the darkness out of sight
Greet your flaws
As you would your charm
With welcoming and open arms

Gentle soul
I see you
How you exist as a cascade of softness
Afraid your good heart will only find company with the broken
Like waves crashing against the shore
Too quickly dissolving into nothing again
But if you are water
You are the same strength
That rises the tides and livens the waves
And though you may break, receding back into yourself
You will emerge again and greater still for it

I make my bed each morning
I flatten the sleep-indented grooves
Of my sheets
With my hands
I brush away the nightmares
The vivid colours, the screams, the tears
I burn esfand as the sun rises
The smoke has kissed my sheets for years
I begin each morning in quiet reflection
Of what new light will bring
With a tidied bed and a clear heart
I hold myself to say, "I am ready to let love in."

The women in my family raised villages
Out of sand and stone
Bore legacies wrapped in sinew and bone
They bled a generation of survivors into being
Seeds that now sprout in foreign plains and far-away cities
Somehow
I remember mountainsides that I've never visited
Their memory is imbedded in my skin
Such is the birthright of my kin
The women in my family were quiet pillars
That still hold me up
That will hold my daughter up
And her daughter up
Until generations of women after me
Tower over the traditions that kept our forebearers
Struggling in the sand

Beautiful woman:
You beam of light
You kiss of fresh air
You feather, you rock of might
You are the earth itself
You are Gaia's heir
Woman, you who carries the world within her
Who birthed it
What can you not conquer?

Patience is the mother of Understanding
The daughter of Kindness
The beginning and end of all things

Grow your dreams muscles and a strong spine
Make them more powerful than all your fears combined

I sink my fingertips into my own neck
Massage the coils of worry building there
The kinks unravel into innocent thought
That curled itself into what ifs and if nots
So powerful are the threads we weave
That from simplicity, anxious narrative is conceived
Yet in time, with writing these worries
In the sphere of our minds
Can manifest pain in our bodies
A malady we cannot hide
So, unravel the knots, reframe your mind
To let go of the broken things
Leave some what ifs behind

Deliverance:
I delivered myself into the light. From darkness.
From a hunger that had less to do with my belly and everything to do with my mind. Years of conditioning. I climbed into a mould that wasn't designed for me. I was hungry to be Her. Worthy. I broke skin trying to fit in, bruised an ego that was already tender like soft fruit.
Deliverance:
I want you to cultivate everything that is love, that is strange, that is fundamental and inconvenient about yourself. I want you to dig your hands into the earth with all the reasons you have been deemed unworthy. I want you to seed your soul into the salt of this world and feed that seed with so much conviction until you burgeon taller than any of the odds that were stacked against you. This is becoming.
Deliverance: Becoming.
Becoming: Freedom.
Freedom: Self.

I will not promise a lover peace that I cannot deliver to myself
That is not love, that is shattering one cycle to bleed another

I am freeing myself of doubt
Of the fear that I have exposed myself
Been raw, bleeding, authentic, me
For the wrong people
I am less concerned with whether they deserved
To hear my story
And more concerned with whether my story needed to be told
And it did, it still does
How they choose to consume my truth is not my responsibility
My purpose is not to control perception

Sometimes we hold the threads of our past
So tightly
That our hands are too full to grasp
The strings meant to weave our future

Be kind and be merciful
The Universe will deliver the judgement

Roses litter the grave I've dug for the woman I used to be
The flowers begin to wilt as I recite my eulogy,
"Goodbye to my first friend, protector, and giving hand
You are the Christ and the disciple, the feet on which I stand
You try to find your voice amidst a symphony of sounds
Dwarfed by their booming protest
Makes your own no less profound
Still, you struggle in your skin, riddled with fear
How easy it would be instead, to simply disappear?
You reduce yourself—your thoughts, your dreams
Until you shrink into a smallness no one can see
But your creativity deserves fawning eyes, your kindness too
I understand you are afraid of revealing the goodness
Because they will see all of you, the bad too, you're convinced
You spend so much time trying to conceal your weaknesses
Your flaws
That you waste the talent that your gifts rest on
Goodbye to my first friend, who shrunk out of need
Goodbye to my first friend, whose hopes are now freed
I am kind to the woman before and what she sowed in seed
Because the woman I am now is her reborn, not lead by fear
But belief."

My womanhood doesn't need to be patrolled by your modesty
I am not more or less human if my skirt
Creeps above my knees
My feminine is divine, not an exhibit for your pleasing class
Chastise your own eyes
If they should follow my hips, my breasts, my ass
I am not here for your consumption
Your control or your reprimand
Veil your sex if my skin weakens its resolve
I am not lesser for the parts of me you choose to crave
Nor the wildness that tempts you in your veins
My body is a God, a temple, a home
And you will bite your tongue before it berates me
For lusts you cannot reign in yourself and leave to roam
Against my walking, heavenly home

The Sun doesn't beg for her love
She lives in love's image and attracts a star in her equal
That is the law of divine attraction:
To be as you seek

Sometimes when the tears do fall, I couldn't tell you why
My heart strings tighten and I soften myself to cry
The water pools in my hands like drops of rain from the sky
I search for answers in my clouds, wherever they hide
The truth is that the body processes pain
Even if we shift our eyes
The body knows the grief we desperately try to disguise
The clouds persist
And darken until we can no longer ignore them
Until the busyness of our day to day no longer out-pours them
The body is a basin, a pool of emotion and cells
It knows that the heart must empty as readily as it swells
Do not protest when the tears do find you
For they are cathartic workers, there to unbind you

Childbirth
When a person who spent nine months
Incubating cells, hopes, dreams
Forgets their suffering long enough
To gift the future and Life itself
Its longing for its sons and daughters
And stewards of progress

Do not let idle gossip settle in your ears
It will displace your thoughts into wickedness
It will build homes where your ancestors sat
Feeding you callousness
And calling it truth
You know well enough
That this nourishes no one

Magic was born first as a woman's right to herself
Her own pleasure, her own energy
Calcified in intention, the root of all sacred effigy
A woman is a priestess in her own right
In the conviction of her power
She swallows sunsets to birth the night
Retiring the woods, water, and children of the day
To sleep and become renewed

The Simorgh flies over our home
Blows our tears away with the thunderous clapping
Of her copper wings
The water sustains her, our salt heavy in the air
Her face is untouched by all the years she has circled the sun
Carrying the pain of daughters she hasn't born into the wind
She looks me in the eye one day, when I cannot stop pouring
When I rival the ocean itself
When my tears cascade like a violent waterfall
And I am drowning as much as I am flowing
She turns my chin up with her wing, gentle and searching,
"You feel you are carrying the oceans of humanity,
but your wounds can only suffer so much salt.
You will find your power here,
in the space that connects you to all beings."
When she leaves again, I feel a tingle in my spine
I touch my shoulder
My finger pricked by the tip of a feather
Emerging from my skin
I have not stood the same since

True sisterhood is about supporting women
As much for their differences as their sameness to us
Never hindering their ability to choose
To shape what freedom means to them
Sisterhood is recognizing that liberation is a flag
Raised in many different colours
Waving against different winds

Some people translate their sadness so often into anger
That they become addicted to it
And forget how to speak in any other language

Every time we raise our fists in anger towards our children
We teach them that love and violence
Feed from the same hand
This beats into their memory, transforming into habit
Habit that becomes the people they choose to love
Into the children they parent
Into societies that are wounded from infancy
Aching with a hunger that you cannot feed
After generations starved

My hair is an unspoken politic
Sprouting vines curly and thick
Framing the flower of my face
Watered with oils and pruned neatly into place
For whom should I flatten my curls to appease?
When they complement the curve of my smile with ease
How can you be so distracted by the coils on my head
That it disillusions you from the words I have said
My hair is an unspoken politic
It greets you across the room
Always growing, tempted but not tamed
Generations of beauty it frames
Whether it suits your tastes I cannot affirm
I will still wear my hair natural, crowned with pride

Some nights I trace my fingers over my skin
Imagine my belly plump, a figure budding within
How I would sustain the two of us, sing to the smaller
How I would walk with a smile
That with each step, might make me feel taller
I would sing and massage oils into the round of its home
The circular motions softening the skin dome
When finally it moves, stretching its legs free
Pressing its palms to my navel, already searching for me
How even in thought, I could love a thing so much
A soul that destiny has yet to touch
What could I say to a child that has yet to arrive?
Except perhaps, "I love you beyond reason or time."

You don't always need to be the champion of the story
The hero
It is enough to survive to tell it
Remembering that survival
Has many different forms and faces
To survive is enough
You are enough

The shadows are teachers too
The light is not the only way
Some healing is found in the dark
Eyes closed to blackness and sought to pray
Illuminating my darkness
I find the irony of the mind's elasticity
That it can snap back from years of trauma
After clinging tight to tortured memory
Still, the darkness is there, even in the light
As the sun rises in the east, half the world is still cast in night
The shadows tell us where our wounds lie, new and old
Where our ancestral scars are buried for us to behold
Fears take soil there, our corruption too
If you never touch the darkness
How can you water the seeds of the unburnt new?

I kiss winter mornings on their frosted cheeks
Snow dusting land, shrubs, and trees
Chickadees cluster to nibble at frozen seeds
On our driveway slicked with ice, slippery to tiny feet
Chipmunks, squirrels, and raccoons
Show their faces by mid-noon
Stealing away crumbs, cheeks packed against the cold
More food is piled outside for our friends to feast
Reminders that we are all children on earth
Both men and little beasts

Raven feathers in the dark of my hair
Moulting into the wind, sprinkled everywhere
Collecting like soot at the base of a fire
Blessing the Earth, purifying the pyre
I wear this hair long down to the small of my back
Like lost ancestors before me who beat down my path
Follow the feathers and the trail that they leave
Generations muted together, the stories we weave
Never a battle between the new and the old
Instead, a reimagining of spaces
To honour the legends we've been told
Traditions are born in time, few are lost
Like trees that survive the winter
While the wildflowers succumb to frost

In another life, I line my eyes with coal
I dip my hands into rose oil
Simmered and sifted into a clay bowl
I massage the oil into my palms, my fingers, my nail beds
Comb it through my lashes, brows, the top of my head
Let it trickle down my face
Past my shoulders and my breasts
Until it tickles my tummy, my thighs, and the rest
Oil seeps into my skin
With the sweetness of a summer rose
My lips are pursed, my skin luminescent and exposed
I drape myself in white fleece, a ceremonial gown
Before I descend upon my own head
A gold embellished crown
The sun rises and sets, by the blink of my eyes
Armies become my footstools, for all their battle-cries
As I walk down royal halls, my hands trace cypress wood
I touch the God and Queen in me
To stand with grace and earn my wool

Breathe life into the parts of you
Left dead, breathless to conform
There is no need to struggle in your own skin
Make peace here, breathe in
You are home

Be sure that what you are demanding of others
You are manifesting yourself, too
A light for a light
Stone for stone
A cup full and embracing cheers in its equal
Not digging wells out of others
Bidding for water with a dry mouth

It took me a lifetime of rising above my demons
To finally find the courage to look one in the face
And see something that I was blind to before:
A wounded child
Seeking comforts the world could not give
Grieving hurts it could not speak
Now, I hold my demons against my chest
Without condemnation—with understanding instead
I let them cry against my skin
I caress their backs with warm hands
I exorcise them out from me
By letting them in

The book of success that you are trying to write
Needs these pages, too
The heartbreak
The failure
The disappointment
They are bound together
I know how you ache to rewrite your suffering
But they make the story what it is
That we can triumph with bruised egos and scraped knees
Is what makes the story worth its weight in gold

Women are everything to me.
Women in sundresses with smiles like blooming daisies.
Women in industry with grease-painted fingernails.
Women who are married to their work.
Women who are married to men.
Women who are married to women.
Women who were not born women.
Women who are undeniably soft.
Women who are unflinchingly brave.
Women who are learning.
Women who teach.
Women who just need to survive the day.
Women with booming voices and steel spines.
Women who are bosses.
Women who are bitches.
Women who aren't afraid to be called bitches.
Women who raise themselves up.
Women who raise their communities.
Women.

Every time you compromise your truth
For the comfort of someone else's lies
A light goes out in a star-filled sky
When adversity pushes your knees down to bow
Forces a narrative into your throat that you cannot swallow
You do what you must to survive
The irony being
That the body lives, but the spirit dies

I have strength written in my bones
I have raised shelters into homes
I guide greatness from meek places
I imprint smiles onto sullen faces
I am a woman looking up to the heavens on high
I am more fire than the sun in the sky
I am daughter to the war-torn
I am the dust settled, foraged gold

You speak in green, so adamant about growing
But the lavender I reply in, is a little more knowing
You tender tiny seeds, anxious to watch them sprout
Overwatering, undernurting
Too often leaving them without
See, the lavender I know, comes with patience and time
It knows the soil must be damp, not soaked
And be fed an abundance of sunshine
Eager hands make for the weaker sow
You cannot rush the leaves before the roots grow
If you want me, you must learn me
Cultivate what strengthens my stem
You cannot coax me into springtime
You must nourish me from within

I talk to my body now
As if my daughter is listening
As if in remarks about myself and my slights
I am educating the next generation of women
On how to love their bodies
With that at stake
Every criticism
Is transformed into love, understanding, light
As it should've been
As it should've been

So many words have become stillborn on my tongue
I find myself lamenting later, grieving them
Shy to say too little, somehow it still seems too much
Heat rises to my cheeks, fires my skin an amber blush
I gulp hot coals, let them collect at the back of my throat
If I have something to say, I may burn
But the world will know

Every time I repress memories of a man's leering
His aggressive sexual prowess
Licked lips, roaming hands
I give him the power to mistake his place again
On the train, an honest mistake
At the party, with drinks surveyed
An illusion, a shapeshifter operating expertly
Grooming the crowd with his fake charm
He disarms them easily
When he stalks after a stumbling girl, he arouses no alarm
He leans in to whisper sex in my ear
Carnal cravings from his mind
He knows how to make me squirm
It's how his words are designed
Those beastly hands follow suit, clawing at their prize
I shoot back despite my unease
The word 'no' a second tongue
Who is he to shrink me down to do as he'll please?
"Keep your hands to yourself," I say
"If you wish to keep them."
I am not fooled; I have met him before
He was a grandfather who groped me at the movies
A young man who followed me at the store
An ex that took what he wanted
Without 'yes' opening the door
I know that beast any time it shows its face

You do not owe anyone the fractured version of yourself
Least of all someone who would cut you down
To make you easier to digest
By standards that no longer feed you

The Scarlet Wednesday before the New Year
We pour out of our homes with a spirit of cheer
Chaharshanbe Suri, a festival of light
Piling brushwood into subtle hills to set afire
The fire is cleansing, a purification tool
An element of the gods, a gift to us too
With the flickering of red tongues over the stacked wood
We prepare to leap over it
Leaving behind the last year's tragedy, its foul mood
I sing,
"Let your redness be mine, let my paleness be yours."
Before I cross the flames, lighter than before

God is in the trees
In the sun
In the sky
In your suffering
In your joy
In the celebration of your success
In the quiet contemplation of your failure
God is with you in this moment
In this breath
When you are eagerly pacing towards the next to-do
Where will you go?
What will you do?
Always digging your hands into life
To pull out more
Looking for God in churches you erect
In accolades that honour your name
You are trying to touch, in frantic movement
What in stillness is yours
You are breathing in all the holiness
You are searching for

The August wind rises and collapses at my feet
A short relief from the torturous summer heat
Sweat collects at the nape of my neck
Water salted like the bow of a shipwreck
I clear my mind and imagine this frame:
An endless sea parting outside my windowpane
I stir in my bed, thinking of that turquoise moon
That romances the sun and overlooks the lagoon
I have adventure in my blood, it has traveled in my veins
In my DNA, for generations beyond this place
Where the unknown conquers others for its dangers
The Salted Woman of me makes friends out of strangers
She embraces life and all its travels
Where she goes, my soul unravels

When the sun rises, there is me
When the sun sets, the same is true
I am the only constant in the cycle of time
I am who I come home to
I choose myself as sure as I do the paint on my walls
The carpet on my floors
The feet that tread upon them
I softly cradle my soles and my soul
Decorating my life with the pleasure
And freedom of knowing
That I am the only one who this life belongs to

Womanhood (noun):
A divinely orchestrated epiphany
That is both born and found
A dawn
A fluidity
A sword
A sheath
A power to protect
A construct to challenge and fight

Power is the presence of love when your anger demands hate

Children are but plants budding in the garden of society
They bloom as they are tended
There are many uncertainties around flower-rearing
So much is beyond our control
Still
We can stand our post
Be a place to lean
Help strengthen their resolve and straighten their stems
We can offer them shade
When the heat threatens to yellow their leaves
We can deliver water to their roots
When arid soil speaks to their thirst
We can even direct their faces to the sunlight
From where they feed
Our duty is to guide their growth
Not decide the plant they will be

Dead the names that fear has taught you
Dislodge them from your ears
Scrub them from your tongue, should you have spoken them
Speak to yourself with such conviction
That the Universe itself is intent on listening
That the Fates create portals to your dreams
Manifest the words you have uttered like gospel
Understanding the power of your intention
Is so mighty that it can alter realities

You look at the stars and feel for your smallness
Not remembering that you are stardust in skin
And you feed from the Sun, a star
How can you convince yourself that you are so disconnected
From greatness, unbeholden to the Universe and its plans
When you are the birthright of the cosmos itself?
You are celestial and belong to the evolution of humanity
This is where you belong
This is where you shine

If I should marry, my vows will proceed my gown, my veil
Even my family tearing up in the pews
My vows will be a living, changing document
What I promise on one day, in the infancy of our marriage
May not be promised under every circumstance
We will change on our own and our dynamic will follow
In years our reflection
Could become so distorted from our youth
When those words were first uttered
So, I will not promise to never go to sleep angry
Because someday a scowl may memorize the lines of my face
Because someday you may deserve my anger
And I will not quell my own feeling for your comfort
If you have wronged me
I will not shrink into the quietness
That falls between married couples
Who have too much to say to one another
But have lost their words to politeness over the years
I will not promise anything but this:
I was a complex, full, and complete person before we married
And I am still –only now I choose to share
The joy of my life with you
I promise that we will argue, we will change, and we will grow
I promise you not forever, but my humanness and my truth
For as long as that sustains us

Frosted glass on cold nights of the past
Memory of coy snowflakes that twirl in the air
Dissolve on my fingertips
Before I can memorize their shape and the patterns
Their icy glass imprints
A lesson I didn't realize the snowfall was trying to teach
How to appreciate people; family, lovers, friends
Come as you are, leave as you'll be
Everything is fleeting, love without capturing

I am sensitive, a little wicked, and brilliant
An old soul with new ambition
Indulgent in myself
Because I dictate my worth to the world
And self-depreciating songbirds
Don't nest at my window anymore
I am a storm worth being named after
A song that catches on your ears
And animates your entire body
I am ecstatic rhythm and movement
A tune you hear and know will be timeless

I am learning to be grateful for my sorrow
My disappointments
They are messengers of my conscious mind
Reminders of when I deserved better
They are architects that build the space to mount a failing
With windows always facing towards the sun and better days

Postcolonial love-notes look like liberation
Without the hashtag
An open hand without an open lens
A dialogue that doesn't position glamourizing allyship
Over actual change
Liberation is uncomfortable
It is unearthing children's bodies across a country that is
In of itself a burial ground
It is understanding we are waves of immigrants fleeing violence
From one nation, only to be complicit in another one's genocide
It is acknowledging red and blue sirens
With fear
Even when we are the victims
Agonizing truths that split us into both sides of the cross
With nails in hand, and nails in our hands
Liberation is unlearning what we were told to be reality
What we had known to be justice
And clearing our eyes and our egos enough to say,
"I am here. I am with you. What can I do?"

Sometimes it is our unravelling
That sews the greatest potential to our fate

Exchange your discomfort for growth
Like a potted plant being rehomed
From a small clay pot, where it found its first sprout
To the soils of a garden, its bloom becoming paramount
Where you are destined
Is greater than where you were rooted

Give yourself abundance and the Universe will follow

When I hold you, I want to feel all of you in my arms
Give yourself to me
Slump your shoulders
Let your spine soften
Abandon your frigid façade
There are so few moments
When we can be naked like this in clothes
Meeting in between the touched and touch-starved
Let me linger in the essence of who you are
That beautiful truth
Divorced from the hardness
That your survival wants you to portray
The imagined weakness
That you apologize for outside of this embrace
Let me take you in
All of you is welcome

My body is not a parking space for the scrutiny of men

The clock loosens its arms, letting them sway to mid-day
In a daydream I have, in the month of May
The spring wind rustles pollen from the top of its stamen
To flow through the air, riding an unseen stallion
Leaving behind a cluster of red eyes and bothered sinus
The pollen finally settles on a grove in the Sun's graces
A fertile plain is more forgiving than God's wrath
Against Eve—no, Adam's sinful path
From an unencumbered horizon, a pasture low to the earth
A creature did sprout and make its birth
I'll never forget her, a goddess of brown and green
With flower veins dropping petals into her hair like rain
She met me in the eye, caught my breath to say,
"You dreamt for a minute, then slept through May."
I still look for her with each spring's arrival
I shake pollen from young stems, inciting her revival
It couldn't be just a dream
She looked at me and gave me meaning
Maybe that's what love is like, with a bit more freedom

The crimson that disgusts you
Could bury you in its wave
But instead, it gives you life, where you expect shame
The Moon demands her blood
And each month we return it to her
In such violence you can find comfort
But for this you are disturbed

You whistle at the sky, in two short blasts
And summon the night, a sapphire cast
The quiet is comforting, save for a few crickets' chirps
The low blow of the wind, like a row of whispers
This is where I meet you: in the silence of things
In the peace that delivers
The truth of beings
In the back of my mind a prayer recites
Though my mouth cannot touch the words and their plight
I lie on the earth, among the meadows and grass
And open my heart to the moments
That have led me to this path
Always searching for sapphire
The moment that God will speak to me
And now that I am here, the language is as foreign as can be
Still, I am not dismayed
I understand between words my fingers fail to trace
That the greatest evidence of the divine
Is imprinted on my own face—God is in all of us
Not the sky, nor a church
God is all of us
With gifts imbued from birth

I am not always so fixated on the idea
Of being loved
I dream about what it feels like
To have someone hold you
And still be free
To disappear the cage
But contain the love
Do this and the bird you admire
Will sing ever more

I clench my fists walking alone at night
My keys squish between my fingers, stand erect for a fight
My eyes dart between trees, at the street
A winding path
I hear an echo of footsteps
But I know I can't look back
So I stiffen a bit and walk faster still
Until I am running into a darkness
I cannot outrun
I have passed my house, the light that was left on
But I don't feel safe there anymore, that comfort is gone
My hand trembles at the lock
There is always something, some way
They can shatter that feeling of safety
I wish I could have Her back
The door to the version of myself that loved the moonlight
Without swallowing a sigh at its shadows
The door to Her is locked
And the nights are longer than they were before

If you want to love me, I want you to love yourself first
You must extend the kindness of each caress onto my body
Onto your own
Feel for your own skin with wonder
The tapestry of life that it is
Write yourself love notes
Carry gifts to your own altar and worship
Pour so much love into yourself
That the excess that showers me
Waters us both

Some days I want to cradle the inner child
The bud of me, stranger to storm
Before a thorn grew from my tongue
I want to heal her so badly, tender her roots and leaves
Give her the space for innocence to grow
Some days I want a multitude of things for her
Acceptance
Healing
Peace
And some days I want vengeance

Eyes betray words
I know when they linger with malice
When they voice questions without sound
My thighs are wide because a country you aren't welcome in
Exists between them
My belly is soft and plump because I value nourishment
Over the mechanics of your aesthetics
My rear is round because it is second daughter to the Sun
See the way heads turn circling it
My perfection does not revolve around your perception

The rustle of trees
Branches that speak in whispers
The Earth shifts through coloured leaves
Time dissolves people and place
But Love is the one that remembers

Pomegranates
Would litter neighbors' yards back home
Shaking themselves free
Stocky spheres tumbling to the ground
With hearty rinds
A rich red that we could only afford on special occasions
Bruised and not quite right in the supermarket
The closest we could gather
The harvest of our hands bobbling in clear bags
From the produce aisle with sticky floors
A little bit of home
So far away from home

Use all your colours on me
The divine paint; your blood, your sweat, your tears
Part my thighs into a masterpiece
The kind you hang over your shoulders, my legs
Not for the walls

You will reach for me with grace
Or I will go phantom from where you thought to touch
I will disappear from a woman of flesh
Into an apparition you can never grasp
A nightmare of longing that haunts you from sleep
Leaving behind only the faint smell of rain and rose water
That too, will be more than you deserve
I know myself too well to demand less
Than the respect I disciple

Remember
Remember to reignite purpose
Not to prolong the pain

The best thing

                                        I can say about grief
                Is that it is a door

The worst thing

                                        I can say about grief
                Is that it is a door

Your kindness
Speaks for you
In the absence of words
It transcends language
It can be translated into hearts without borders

Plant flowers and thoughts where you wish to see them grow

Winter frosted my lips into cold silence
Covered my face with snow
Left me barren fruit or leaf
Unlike the life that once grew out of me
Silence
How much evil relies on silence
Depends on a storm of fear
To make survivors out of women
Who have already survived so much
My voice is a summer carnival now
It colours the air
It demands to be heard
I will not suffer in my solitude
Resign myself to fruitless months, years, decades
So that your comfort is unbothered by seasons

I grew up humbled under a cloud of shame
Yet somewhere deep inside me rang,
"They will know my name."
A fumbling mess with a matted mane
A foreign lineage, too-hard-to-pronounce name
Still, my bones said,
"They will know my name."
Snake-eyed friends and hostile strangers
A mental haze fraught with danger
Damned I'd be, to hold on and say,
"They will know my name."
A drum inside
This frail heart beat
That summons me to my feet
When I am meek, unsure of myself
I remember that within, I hold my wealth
I am bounteous
I am brave
And I promise you this:
You will know my name

Sometimes I have so much sadness living in me
That I sour my own fruit
Before they mature from the branch
So, I sit outside in the summer rain
When the sun is warm against my skin
The water that pours rushes to the earth
Just as quickly as it came, dissolves from its birth
And that is so much of how I feel
Fleeting like a seasonal wind
My tears roll back into my eyes
Almost as soon as their journey down my cheeks begins
I don't pour the way I used to
Something has blunted me from my pain
I don't pour the way I used to
I'm a vanishing summer rain

Forgive the wanting part of you
That knocked on locked doors, waiting
That swallowed your pride and words that needed to be spoken
That burned in fires you yourself fanned flame for
That knew less back then
Than you do now
Witness this feeling
Host anger and hurt
Host sadness and heartbreak
Host every feeling that comes over you in your humanness
Give them time, empty them space
Let Forgiveness in, to envelop you
And fill the cracks of the broken places
A gold in porcelain
Holding you stronger than before

Womanhood is the collective experience
Of splitting yourself in two
And becoming whole
I would not have survived it
Without the women who celebrate me
My life is defined by womanhood and sisterhood
For it, I am full

I am reshaping the society of my thoughts
To call my dreamthings destinations instead
A dream can be a feckless place, fragile to touch
But a destination is rooted in reality
That it is only a matter of time, of distance
Before you get there
More than an imagined reality, a waiting one
So that every day as I toil
I am working to inch closer to where I need to be
A destination, not a dreamthing
A destination, not a dreamthing

I hide cigarette butts under my tongue
Ashamed I've been anxiously smoking them
The starlings perch above me, stare curiously
Wondering how this fixation started and when
I tell them my father smoked two packs a day
Before I was born
And the tar can still be wrung from his lungs
When I get nervous, which is often these days
I paint, I feed the birds, and I smoke into dawn
The Moon doesn't worry for me like the starlings do
They inspect my plumage, the ash in my hues
They tell me stories, eat seed and nectar from my hand
They ask about the nightmares
The imprint of an old wedding band
If I delve into my sorrow and fall in too deep
They spread their metallic-sheened wings and uplift me
And if I somehow sleep through the night
They knock on my door in twos
People may forget you, but the starlings never do

My sister kisses me on both cheeks
And makes me promise to never turn them
Not again
Not anymore
Not for anyone
So many handprints have blistered my skin
Connected welts from closed fists, bruised blue
And open hands
I have learned less about mercy from them
And more about the kind of evil
That preys on kindness
I'll turn my cheek no more
Suffering will not be my second name

Worship the storms for the rain you needed

I once had a dream after an old friend died
That she would be reborn in the water as a restless tide
Now every time I look to the sea
I catch the blue of her eyes
I sit in the sand by the shore
Watching her roll towards the sunrise
Her daughter never knew
How much joy her mother brought
By the ring of her laughter, the innocence of her thoughts
She died when her daughter was just a baby
Not a few months old
Now she lives eternal with the mothers of her past
In waters that wave and fold, with the salt of Everlast

Every year
I ask Life to feed me lessons
To open my eyes to realities I hadn't dreamt before
And each year, without fail, I learn, and she humbles me
Through tragedy or success
Elation or sorrow
She delivers me

Steer your thoughts like a voyager boat
Claiming the sea
While wrestling the undertow
Reality is not clear skies
Or sedated waves
Not that Poseidon would have them that way
The liquid road is paved by change
As in life, it cannot be subdued by rage
Or bent by anger
Or whittled to shape by anxious thought
It simply is a mutable clay of water and salt
A knowing hand can travel far
With patience and an acceptance
For things as they are
Move as life moves, forget your rigid spine
Plans will unravel, flow through your fingers
In a flash of time
Your becoming is the acceptance
That transforms glass into sand
Reduces sharp shards into powder in your hand
Welcome the waves as they come
Flow too as they flow
Sometimes the only way to survive is to become

Hair is history
A bed of cloud
A road of silk
A knotted roadmap
Of culture and kin

A bird struggles, drowning
In a shallow bath
Other birds think it is bathing
And simply fly past
But I know what dying looks like
When you ache to clutch onto light
When the air from your lungs empty
When your body recedes from life
I cup my hands before it and notice its twisted leg shake
Its shuddering small body
Soon warms against my skin
I look for this in people
Though the signs are less clear
Death can live in smiles
And still be far too near
An emptiness can live in your household
Or a party filled to the brim
With a bustling group of bodies
With one or more souls adrift
It's the eyes that cannot escape me
Even if everything else rings true of cheer
I know how that darkness tunnels its way
Into a hollow basin, collecting tears
Every time I meet someone
Or check in on an old friend
I think of Alice who tunneled too deep

And fell into marveled existence
But in this world, things are simple
I see only a bird writhing against the water
Its beak once parched with thirst
I think of that bird
Its struggle with willed wings
It seems the fight is winding down
Yet each feather raises and persists
If I could see you wholly
And the battles that you grace
The ones that batter your insides
That do not translate on your face
I would give you my strength in cupped hands
A guiding word, anything, and all that I have
So that you never find yourself drowning
In a shallow bath

My heart has been suspended
In a jar of my own musing
It floats in a brine of my tears
That no one else was using
I preserve my heart on a shelf
So high that even I cannot reach it
I watch it wither in memory
The salt of my failed teachings
How was I not wiser?
How could I come so far only to regress?
The questions circle the drain
And all the same, disappear into darkness
Still, that puckered heart beats
A pickled muscle in sour water
It ripples chants of forgiveness
Through the glass in which it's cornered
Cut from my chest and displayed in clear
The heart can recover from anywhere
Inspired then, I reach up higher
My spine straightening into an even tower
I take my heart back to its home
A bony cage to speak from
A heart cannot live on a shelf
No matter the sins it's acquired
Forgive the heart as the heart forgives
With no reservations required

Growing pains
From finding my own skin
A marriage of my own making
And what I inherit from my kin
Finding the right fit
Of who I am and who I will be
So much tension between the shoulders
Of self-made prophecy
I am my family in ways I cannot escape
I am myself in the paths I pave
This skin was made to stretch
Its shape will not stay static for long
If I evolve from this becoming
It will follow along

Hope can pull you from a pit of despair
Just as disappointment planted you there
The knowledge that the end is not The End
That so much can be born again
Is only reason to reclaim
Your power to rise from a second flame
The human spirit is a phoenix with feathers red and blue
And sometimes we must sacrifice our burning
To emerge anew

I breathe kindness into my lungs
Into the air
So that the trees and plants take what I spare
Their leaves develop a proud sheen
Their colouring becomes a more lustrous green
In turn the oxygen they produce
Is lovingly imbued
Soon, that trickles onto the birds
Who feed and rest in the wooded structures
Somehow, in time, their song is changed
To a more harmonious tune
That lives in the wind and heals the Earth's blue

The goal isn't always to see through the fog
To know yourself is clarity enough
That awareness will guide you
Be a vision for you where eyes cannot follow

A friend once described my hair lovingly
As a bird's nest
I remember how my nose wrinkled at the thought
Assuming it was said in jest
How disgusting, I grimaced
Imagining how the mop of curls atop my head sat
That he could look upon them and see
A tangled airy mat
Then, on a summer day
I watched the sun bleed from morning until mid-day
In the blistering heat
A bird flew with a twig in its mouth joyously
To and from its nest, it collected eager mount
Making a home for its unlaid eggs
Where its children would sprout
The nest was piled lovingly
Each wooden piece expertly woven
To ensure the integrity of the home the bird had chosen
Streaks of light still shone through
Illuminating a myriad of earthy hues
It was a beautiful mess for an eye untrained to see
The beauty of the natural order, that springs so lovingly

Do not allow your fear and suffering
To be the only meal you feed from

The swaying of branches
The singing of birds
The flow of the river
The orchestra of Earth
Search for it in the quiet
In the quiet, the divine speaks
It can be heard from the rooftops of skyscrapers
Just as in country meadows that are barren peaks
Holiness is not a lined face, as wisdom is not innate in age
You are no further from God lying in the gallows
As you are when settled above the mountain range
Anything sold to the contrary, is the sale of illusion
Of belief
Rather than the heart of life which you seek
So, start from where you stand
The journey is now
You are just as connected to greatness in this moment
As the brain beneath your brow
Anywhere you must travel
You must visit with your mind first
This is the ultimate subscription
This is the reason for your birth
I memorize the footprints that trailed the paths before me
I understand the weight of each step

If I feel unsure in my voyage
I will know I am not alone for my trek
Your ancestors have more to give you
Than the spirit of their pain
There are lessons in the paths they beat down for you
Gifts still to gain

Fight the instinct to deprecate yourself
In jokes that make your own skin crawl
Because you have been taught
To bloom against the wall
Where there is only shade, no sunlight, no water
Even in the grey of this imagined land
You feel your heart sink further
In the pit of your belly, like a seed planted low
If you stifle yourself, you'll never have to grow
In kind, you'll never suffer to be seen
In a confident garden among the greens
There is comfort in the wall
I know, I've lived there too
But that murky existence pales your vibrant hues
To be seen and to be vulnerable
To admit your worth to the world
Can send shivers down your stem and rattle your roots
But that is when you must plant yourself firm
You have intelligence and talent
A voice worth being heard without stall
You may never evict your worries from your mind
But you must live outside the wall

I served a man, hand and foot
Crystallized his fantasies into the ring
He eventually slid onto my finger
Met his family twice
In the flesh
In the trauma that made him
I withstood his pain when it became mine
A slammed door, a raised voice, a bruised wrist
I served a man, 500 feet
At all times
Zero contact
Court order

I work day and night
So that my parents' dreams for me
Aren't reserved reality for when they sleep
I work day and night
So that my parents' dreams for me
Don't die with them

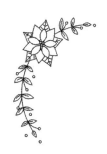

Abandoning yourself
A divorce of the most sacred union
When you honour others above yourself
Stunting your own spirit
Service and goodness to the world
Is beauty
But to break your back
Bent on the demands of someone else
Is a crime to the personal psyche
So come home to yourself
Your own needs and desires
The selfless may be followed like prophets
Yet just as easily become martyrs
Come home to yourself
And no matter how far you go
You will not wander

How much of you lives in the half-truths
That split away to become society's muse

Worship is more than prayer
To love is to worship
To dance is to worship
To serve others is to worship
Connecting to a higher power is simply
An extension of creating beauty from any circumstance

I have caught a holy man's eyes
Admiring the God that slopes down my chest
For all his piety
He could not peel his lids from my breasts
For his lust, he chastised me
A girl no more than 13
If your eyes should wander my body
With ill intention, a carnal craving
It is not my modesty you should be surveying
You will not pervert my body from existence
Or from my own allowance
Think instead, why your eyes should bleed
For a girl, no more than 13

Speak with an educated tongue
And an open mind
If you are humbled into silence
Take lesson
There is no fault in missed knowledge
The dagger comes from choosing not to learn
Clinging to ignorance like a seeping wound

I am so dedicated to my becoming
That my former selves
Daydream about the woman I am today

Too many women I love
Have been branded selfish
For having an identity
Beyond servitude

I want someone who understands
That my heritage colours my view of everything
It informs my loving
It narrates my workday
It will raise my children
(If even in gentler ways than it raised me)
It is the seen and unseen parts of me
Imperfect, intangible, priceless to knowing me

Sometimes people become so romanced by their own fiction
A seduction of events as they should be
Rather than as they are
That you cannot pull them from their lust for half-truths
The world that they have invented
Feeds a craving for order
That the uncertainty of this reality cannot
But how many perceptions exist in this small world
In this frame we know as reality
How much does it differ among minds
Perhaps even singular realities split when spread among hands
There may not be anything to rationalize or condemn
The moment we present a truth, it is already gone
Whatever realness we survey is altered by our race, our means
The relativity of our dimensions in poverty clashes
Against those of great wealth
We can live in the same world, in very different worlds
And even among the elite
Race makes some pockets fuller than others
Groomed by the lie that we all have the same hours
That our very zip code does not determine life expectancy
We may challenge the odds yet never avoid them
Until the supremacy created is destroyed
Until the work is done by those in power that benefit
From feeding us tall tales

Sometimes it feels like too much to bear and we are starved
For an escape, a fiction of filtered gaze
A seduction for things as they should be
Rather than as they are

My softness was battered by the callous of the world
My anger is not for jabs and jeers as a grown woman
She can take them
My anger is for the little girl who should not have
That girl is everything to me, she is who I protect
The girl who came to and from school with bruises
Who sought comfort and found cruelty
Who battled words and fists without armour
Who could not escape the violence because it followed her
As sure as the sun
Whose softness, battered
Somehow persisted, blossomed still
Despite the thorns she'd been fed

My body has been a canvas for scars
I am amazed by how far I have traveled in myself
How I multiplied from a single cell, grew from a babe
Who knew no more than milk and my mother's arms
Into a child whose mind was as mischievous
As it was inventive
Finding new ways to collect scrapes and bruises
From misadventure
(And sometimes not)
How my skin stretched further still to house the woman
I am today
I wrap my arms around myself, happy to be home

The Sky is not always married to the Sun and the light
In the same way the Sky is not always married
To the Moon and the darkness she summons
Life reflects these phases
It gives us pause in our joy
Lament for tragedy we have endured and will again
In the same way, it fosters hope to seed from our sorrow
Knowing that goodness will return

You cannot beat your spirit down
Into betterness
Be kind to yourself in the process
Love the version of yourself that exists in this moment
She needs tenderness to grow

Do not rush your healing for the comfort of others
It takes a moment to maim something
An instant to break it
It can take a lifetime to restore it
So many of us are walking wounds in skin
Displaying our brokenness in our dysfunction
Yearning for scar tissue to reform us
To dull the ache
Of where tragedy first kissed us into fragments

Some despair is so deep
That it tunnels its way down the human soul
And on the other side there is no more grief, but freedom

The Heartbreak was my second birth
That I should be weighed by a man's impression of my worth
I am not Adam's rib brought to life
A bearing station for children, a would-be wife
Yes, children are a blessing
And marriage can be a magical union
Yet that I should crumble if I choose myself above these
Is a sour delusion
I am enough as I stand
A woman unincumbered by the demands of man
A woman of ambition, with great love in my heart
Not cut into a role where I cannot choose the part

I am a settler on stolen land
I speak the invader's tongue
I benefit from the exit wounds that we now call cities
I am an immigrant's daughter who saw freedom here
Without its past
Now I must reconcile the two realities:
That I am privileged beyond words to have escaped
The violence that plagues my ancestral home
And that I am, without exception
Responsible for demanding justice for the violence
That built my colonist one

If my silence
Makes me more likeable
It is not my voice
But your intolerance
That must be quieted

A bird blew past my window
Adrift in the wind
A few leaves kicked up in its image
And soon returned to the trees
A moment became two, became many, became hours
A moment of reminiscing in spring
A season passed into passing summer
A person can become so fixated on the things
That evade their grasp
A bird, a job, a lover, a moment from the past
Adrift in the wind, they too soon disappear
Allowing themselves to fade into the winters
Missing new moments as they appear

My soul is a garden teeming with flowers and trees
Birds nest in the greenery, visited by eager honeybees
Sometimes I choose what grows here
I sow the seeds of thought
Often what blooms is inherited
Wildflowers in the shape of genes I forgot
Though I cannot control all the plant-things
That make up this garden
Rooted so deeply in my earth
I can control what gets fed and grows up from my dirt
Kindness flowers here
Judgement, too
The first I water
The second, I leave to rot in root

Women have burned for less than I resolve to do in a day
Been stoned into erasure from family history
For what now is merely considered existing
Been hung with recycled noose
Wet with the tears of their inconsolable fathers
To enjoy the freedoms that I live
Means catching a glimpse
Of the rights, the basic dignities that many miss
A world over
Where I see the sun rise from my bedroom in the west
It has already risen in the east, hours before
From barred windows

The woman you are comparing yourself to
Does not exist in the real world
She has been cinched and edited from her truth
Contorted into a brand commodity
Designed by someone else's hand
To disappear human imperfection
They have injected into her whatever trend they've decided
Will consume your eyes this month
The caricature of a woman robs both you and her
The peace of living in your own skin
If tomorrow you decided, hand in hand
To reject the fantasy curated for you to attain
Empires that watched over your adolescence with judgment
Whose voices only got louder as they began critiquing
Your womanhood
Would crumble at your feet

If all my life
I had charged
For the emotional labour
Of raising a man from under my breast
I could afford to buy back
All the promises his ego did not let him fulfill

Imagine crossing the horizon
With blood-soaked footpaths
Only to be labelled sloth
When you finally seek rest
The world is not divided by East and West
It is divided by humanity and corporation

Chemistry is a dance of energy
If you are fluent in how my body talks
If you can meet me in the unspoken places
What is private to the world
Will become yours intimately in time

Sometimes I avoid speaking with my father
Knowing our politics will claw at each other
Knowing that our time together is precious
Wanting to savour what remains sweet between us
For our similarities and not our differences
What has grown together rather than so far apart in years
I am conflicted by the conflict that is born from how we think
How sometimes we seem so close to aligning
Only to diverge again
But avoidance has taken years from us
So much silence has sat in place of our conversations
That we are alien to communicating at all
How in the process of trying to preserve our relationship
It has all but dissolved, unspoken
Perhaps the only way to love one another
Is to confront the discomfort
And still find a way to fold into each other
Embracing that we are two very different people
With fragments of the same heart

Women create art out of everything
Life itself is a woman's painted landscape
Think of how she transforms cells into arms and legs
A beating heart, eyes bursting with colour
How she rearranges her very organs to make room
For her master work
Shaping a soul out of fleshy clay
She stretches a single note of a heartbeat
Into a lifelong symphony
She grows communities like they are an extension
Of her own ornamental garden
She is creator of, and the art itself

Meditate on memories of tenderness
Let softness envelop your body
Find peace in this moment
Where the forgiveness lives
Where wars have been settled like dust on the earth
Where all is made clear in the silence

Wildflowers grow on my arms, my legs
They grow between my brows and above my lips
Sometimes I prune their leaves
If they are crowded and persistent
I pull them from their root
I am barren land for a time
Until the spring of a new week has them growing again
However they form, I speak kindly to them
Knowing they are an extension of me
And the country that is my existence

The greatest love of my life
Is not another person
But the echoing of my own soul
The greatest love of my life is Endurance
Survival
The willingness to embrace Life
Regardless of what she has taken from me

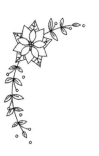

The aching is not the only soundtrack to your recovery
It is the preface to its blessings
Your recovery sounds like all the prayers
You didn't hear for your healing
Torn from the lips of every person
Who believes you can exist outside of your addiction

Resilience still requires rest
Healing speaks from anger
Peace is born from practice, not circumstance
Love is a natural reflex and a learned behaviour
Perhaps above all, love is the small part
Of our individual humanity that touches holiness

Turn off your phone
Peel out of your clothes and shower
Wash the day off you
Strip your sheets, too
Wash everything
Dust the halls and the shelves from the stale energy
That perches there
Open the window and let fresh air circulate the space
Burn the esfand and lavender
Light a candle for the fire inside of you that still burns
Dab rose water behind your neck, on your wrists
Sink into fresh clothes, anointed
Roll into a bed of pressed linens, lighter than the day
And its heaviness had promised
Settle your eyelids for sleep and rest
Truly, peacefully
This is how you care for yourself after a massacre
With your own two arms cradling you

My father plants a peach tree
In the middle of our front yard
Its fruit grow small and supple
In the summer heat they prevail, uncharred
When later we find a dead baby robin
Fallen from its nest housed on a lithe branch
I bury it just below, on the same plot of land
Its mother watches eagerly and builds a new nest across the way
Her songs echo back to the peach tree
Where her first egg she did lay
I arrange flowers from the garden
Over the baby's resting place
When I close my eyes to say a prayer
I can see my own mother's face
I continue chanting prayer and the round of her belly
Suddenly comes into frame
When she miscarried my brother
Her body ached for days
She transformed those years of longing
Into days of me and my sister's play
Transformed her grief into softness
The science of her mothering
So I close my eyes for the baby bird and the unsung son
With her grace guiding my words to God
Both torn from this world before they could taste
The sweetness of a peach on their tongues

My smile springs back
Elastic
In the face of my tears
Gratitude can be seen from dark places
Like a night rain that refuses to obstruct the stars

The little chin hair that pricks
At my softness, my conceived femininity
Stands black and defiant on the edge of my face
Each moment it lives there, I feel it grow longer
Until I am convinced it has grown so long
That I can comb it back with the rest of my curls
How something so small can command
So much of my attention
Can transform into a shard of glass, sharp
Cutting out of me and a womanhood I hesitate to step in
Bleeding from it the fragility of what they have designed
What is a woman if she is not hairless, soft, delicate
Maybe
Anything she wants to be

Cast aside what your fears have told you
The Sun will rise again tomorrow
You can try again under her light
Illuminated, your scars are maps
Designed to remind you
That you will be repaired
That healing is always the final resting place

When the mind forgets
The heart remembers
That is all humanity is:
Blood dancing through pulled heartstrings

Moonchild
You are wiser than the mistakes behind you
Brighter than the sun above you
Wherever you go
Whatever you do
You will have the entire sky in your corner
Holding you up

Beauty is my religion
It shapes my perception of the world and the people in it
Wrinkles are beautiful
Making our elders gods
Kindness is beautiful
Making healers, creators, sweet souls, my priests
Recovery is beautiful
Making our suffering, those fighting addiction
Like living prophets
Unbridled hope is beautiful
Making our children disciples of life's eternal plan
An image of ecstatic beauty

I asked God to lead me to the river
That would cleanse me of the past, do the healing
And he sent me on a road back to myself
With water on my mind

Your healing must be firmly rooted in the future
So that the turbulence of the day to day
The disappointments of your environment
Do not untether you from the growth that is your becoming

Unify the voices of criticism in your mind
Into a single voice that encourages, empowers you
By reminding them
And yourself
That you feed the tongues that lash back in judgement
That they will starve without your attention

I tattooed a moth onto my wrist
After I broke free from a love that had imprisoned me
As I rattled shackled, trapped in my chains
I was becoming the iron encircling me
It flowed through my veins
I couldn't help but remark
Something had changed within me
Dimmed my internal spark
While the fire still burned somewhere
It became shallower still
Could barely keep me warm
Against the cold drifting in from my windowsill
But I kept looking for the light
Until in freedom, I dug it out from me
I tattooed the moth as a reminder
That we are both our best when we are free

Be the kind of person who prays for other people's fortune
That celebrates victories that aren't theirs
That loves for the sake of loving
That lives walking in the footsteps of the Creator herself

If you are a healer
You still need your medicine, your healing
If you are a giver
You still need your gifts, your receiving
Nourish as you are nourished
You can be the image of love itself
And still need your heart cradled, tenderness

I drink my coffee in the morning by the window
With my eyes towards the sun
Drink sliding down my throat
With the warmth of a burning star
I blink back tears, treasuring this moment of peace
This place
Standing here
In my father's kitchen
Alone in my quiet
Save for a kettle bubbling beside me
In another house, very different from ours
But altogether the same
Bombs are descending upon their neighbors
Thinly-covered roofs are leaking rain
The sun hides itself from their suffering
Hidden away by smoke clouds polluting their lungs, too
I am grateful for this moment always
When I am awake enough to taste my coffee
And know that it is more than just quiet
That sweetens the privilege of standing here

I am the rind, the seed
I am the fruit that I bleed
I am the water, undiluted
Pulled from flowers I have fruited
I am the refined final product, packaged for the masses
I am the poured nectar they spill into their glasses
I am everything I have been
Unashamed of what I will become
Returning to the earth as compost
Feed for another generation

Plant your seeds
The water will come

Jelly daggers
Flailing against my skin
How my resolve can twist iron
To writhe from within
My smile is my armour
My laughter, a heavy shield
My good spirit is the mightiest sword that I can wield
You can splinter wood into a thousand pieces
And you can melt metal into nothingness still
But you will find yourself ill armed
Against open, giving hands and a determined will
So, when the battle of words comes
Another crisis yet avails
It is the simple-hearted who among us, will prevail
Not lost to the shrapnel of idle gossip and ugliness
I know in sincerity where my thoughts will rest
So be soft, little one
Shed your cunning disguise
Give way to your joyfulness
Rise to your idyllic high
You are different from the others
I know, I am too
But what makes you different
Is what shapes a soul from unfinished dreams
Into something brave and new

Beloved,

I want you to know that I am proud of you. For the woman you are and the woman you are becoming. I know you think you are behind. I know that some days the comparisons are all too easy to make. I know that other days the grief can sit on your chest and make it hard to breathe. You don't need to chastise yourself. Or ask why the sadness is still here. We are so accustomed to compartmentalizing our feelings that we forget we are allowed to have them sometimes. We alienate ourselves from the truth. That pain lingers. That some losses can't be filled. And it is okay that they ache sometimes. Because that means that it was real. We've also condemned ourselves to believe that the grief is a monster in a box. That we are trapped inside with it. And that we need to conquer it to be free. But the truth is that grief is water. We need it. We need to grieve so we know we loved. To remember we are still loving. That things—that people, time, life itself—is precious. Grief is not a monster you have to fight. It is the water you will grow from. It is a reminder to nourish yourself and live as dearly as you can. While you can. Because everything evaporates. Is fleeting. And that's what makes life beautiful.

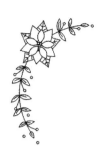

How hunger feeds revolutions
You must be starved for your own evolution to touch it

You are a marbled sky
The lovechild of marriage dark and light
You speak in clenched fists and mourn quietly
Because anger keeps moving like industry
Whereas sadness rests solemnly
And you are too tired to be tired
Have too much to accomplish to sit with the pain
Even when your marble sky
Loses its light and darkens with rain
It is easier to wield anger
To spit lightning and land a thunderous blow
But eventually the busiest day will come to an end
And then where will your heartbreak go?

Take time to listen to your body
To nourish it, cleanse, and soothe it
Run your own hands over your skin
Knead over the knots you can reach
The nerves you can tender
See the static crackle
In the moments your body, electric
Feeds off the sensation of touch
Receptors indiscriminately signaling calm
A moment of safety
A mothering you can deliver to yourself
Your body is your family, your neighbor
The house itself
A collection of cells yearning for connection
Fed in quiet moments of dedicated self-love

Other women's success is my celebration
Envy does not elevate me
It only alienates me
From the person my mother raised me to be

Speak to yourself softly
Gently enough to preserve the daisies
That pour out of your mouth
Speak to yourself in the flowering grace you offer others
Because you are just as sweet and deserving
Be the woman to yourself that you have been for others

Howl what you want
Mothers before you did not swallow their tongues
To survive your legacy
So that you could shrink the wolf in your voice
And not speak what you need

I wonder sometimes
Why it took meeting us
For so many of our fathers to stop
Being the kind of men we are told to avoid
Why were their mothers not enough
Why were their lovers hollow from them
Why was any woman on the street not a lesson
In not just how to be a man
But how to be human

I give birth to a poem three times
Once in my mind, fluttering behind my eyelids
Once in my mouth, silken on my tongue
Once in pen and paper
With parts of me that linger on the page
I met the manifestation of myself today the same way
Once in my mind, a nightmare of him leaving
Once in my mouth, hearing myself whisper, "Stay."
Once in pen and paper, letters I wrote, then burned
To a man whose brokenness cut into me
Made me a poet
Made forgiveness my north star
Guided my love in all the flaws he deemed unlovable
Reflected me
Redirected me
To a mirror of myself that births art without begging
For beauty, for praise
Knowing enough to appreciate prose
And people
Are more beautiful
When they gravitate to you naturally

Little blossom
How much adversity you have endured
In the wake of your bloom
What makes you beautiful is a slap in the face
To every opinion rooted in prejudice, in the past
Your growth a reminder
Of what deserves to be watered, the future
It is not your life's purpose to defend who you are
Your job is to flower despite the weeds around you
Who think they can decide
Whether you belong in the garden

When you offer me a rose, lover
Offer me the thorns, too
Do not let me become seduced
By wafting fragrance and crimson hue
Without knowing what it will mean
When my hands are clasped around its stem
Offer me a rose, with its thorn
And let me decide
What I can hold

If loss should ever darken your door
And cast its shadow into an unending night
Look for the stars
There are always stars to guide you

Some hammers in life broke me while others built me
The tools were the same
Only I changed how they touched me

Woman born, woman forged
Feminine shifting in between
Your hands are my hands in sisterhood
Through different lands and borders unseen
I will protect you, fight for you
This is what it means to be family

The truths that carve out the otherness on your face
In your mind and in your speech
Will shape you
So that you can embrace the art of not fitting in
It will teach you to walk between worlds
The life your zip code ordains, down to a science
And the power you thought wasn't meant for you
Welded into the crown
You will someday lower onto your brow
On reclaimed land

Do not become so consumed with the idea of a relationship
That you forget your ambition
Your own goals, your dreams
To stifle yourself in the name of love
Is the opposite of love's doctrine
If you cannot grow together
You are lingering in the wrong soil

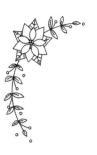

You are not responsible
For how your message of love
Is translated from your tongue
And twisted into someone else's ears
As hate
You can only control your words
How another person's traumas become their perception
Of your message
Is not your burden
Relieve yourself of this worry

Intimacy is not compatibility
Passion is not compatibility
Love, even, is not compatibility
Experience moments and people
With open hands
Clinging only to the beauty of memory
Knowing that a single spark
A fierce burning
Doesn't kindle flames eternal
Isn't always meant to
Yet we can still treasure
That for a time
It brought us in from the cold
And fed us warmth

The footprints of you loving yourself
Sink thick in the sand
Next to the feet of your guides
Who walked alongside you with pride in their hearts
And the gratitude of your daughters' daughters
In their steps

Children
Are
The
Eyes
Of
God

Do not punish your mind
For the time it needs to rest
We are bombarded with human suffering
To exist in the chaos of today
Is to subscribe to wounds harvested
From someone else's body
To labour trauma gestated in different countries
Born into our collective consciousness
Through news of unrest
That rears restlessness
So much so that we forget the hurt
That kept us up before we saw our hearts reflected
In the pain of a stranger

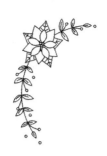

Sisterhood is defending the sacred feminine
From the patriarchy
From white supremacy
From anti-blackness
From xenophobia
From anti-Semitism
From ableism
From fatphobia
From homophobia
From transphobia
From neurodivergent prejudice
From every spear and battle
That aims to conquer what a woman is
Deciding who she will become
Is reduced to less a person
And more a product of war

On a lover's holiday
I wake up with no lover in my bed
Just a burnt candle
Two wicks already spent
I tell myself that love has left here
That it has abandoned me
Left me without grace
Until I see a friend's smile
And find only love reflected in their face
I love my friends
And they love me
The same echoes true
For my family
I love my life
Experiences I've yet to have
Still, I have passion
To guide my path
Love is all around me
It lives in me, too
Love is more than a lover
It begins with you

You do not owe anyone
A version of your life that suits their vision, their desires
Their closeness to you is not the rent they pay
To live in that reality
Because at the end of the day
You must live there alone

When your parents speak to you about their past
With tears on their tongues
Memory creeping up their throats
Ready to pour out from their mouths
But instead, they curl their lips to say
"That's just how things were."
Recited plainly, with prepared conviction
Their resolve shaking at the sight of you
Your open arms, your knowing eyes
The same eyes you inherited from them
The vision that comes from somewhere higher
In those moments the image of your idol
The genesis of your anger, too
Dissolves into a child that nursed you
Before they tended their own wounds
A child that is still hurting
That yearns for the forgiveness it takes
To crash into your arms
And feel, if even for a moment
The peace you found amidst the chaos
The peace they could not deliver to you

Understand that your water is precious
That as much as you are the rain
You are the earth it feeds
Your passion isn't about destruction
It nourishes what it is meant for
And washes away what is not

Accept that your name will sour
Someone else's tongue
It does not matter how well-intentioned
Your sweetness was
We are all villains
In someone else's story
What matters most is that we live with honour
And are guided by kindness
So that however we are written
In someone else's book
We can be at peace
With how we are written in our own

Mourn what is lost
Celebrate what is to come
Dust marries dust
As red rivers run
If the phoenix denied its burning
It would never moult into its own sun
To be reborn is to dead who we were before
And trust that the fire will reveal us

I grace my sadness with levity
Having learned curled fists
Do not challenge my depression
So much as they become instrument to it
Playing many different tunes
That eventually all sound the same
Like different faces made from the same plaster
Forming the same shapes
I sit with the grief until my backside numbs
Only then do I rise to my feet
Ignoring the existing trumpets of orchestra
Sadness demands sadness
Before it can be conducted into a note of change

Decorate your home with fond memories
Create a sanctuary where you can find peace
The world outside can be a whirlwind of cunning
You deserve a safe reprieve

The changing room light illuminates little else
Except flaws
The dimples on my legs and butt
The scar that lives along my jaw
I simmer my heavy breath
Pants from struggling into pants too small
Imagining I am the only one struggling
In these rows of changing room stalls
How crowded the space becomes
When critique shows up in the room
Crowding you into the corner
Where the panic ensues
The dimples don't dissolve, and the scars won't retire
Greater still, I notice, the incomparable 'spare tire'
In the next stall, I hear a muffled sob
A girl my age fiddles with the lock
Pours out as readily as the tears that streak her face
Wearing a silk green dress accented with lace
I poke my head out to see her
And her mother that instructs her to twirl
For all the mutterings of callousness
I see only a beautiful girl
So, I step back into my changing room
To gaze at the body I monstrously tore apart
And see only a body, five feet, six inches tall

The storm will rewrite you

I have potential for greatness
Because everything I do is a seed planted with love
And love is the greatest resource on earth
The dearest form of nourishment
As we are restored to our bloom by it

The soul is a budding tree
Absorbing neighbouring philosophies
Your roots touch roots
With the people you choose to exchange energy
They feed your bark to weather storms
Or crumble your leaves with hostility
If you are only as tall
As wise
As awakened
And as fruitful as your friends
Do you stand among giants?

Do not ask the thorn why it pricks you
Ask yourself why you choose to cling to it
Why when the rain pours, your roots dance
Nature cannot be tempted from tradition
Yet we can choose the pain we condition

What is meant for you
Will raise you up
The same way your elders
Forfeited their shoulders
So you could stand higher upon them
This is the divinity of love, the ascension

When the light within you shines bright enough
It becomes the light around you
Nurse your fire and it will keep you warm
Nourish what aches to be fed and make clear your path
By living your truth this way
You illuminate not just your way
But you impart sun into those around you
Who shine in reflection of your rays
Emancipate yourself from darkness
And light will find every soul you love

The sun will rise again
You will be washed
Your heart will be whole, my friend
The heartbreak soon forgot
The mourning will not curate every morning
At night you will find rest despite the restlessness you feel
You will make peace from your broken pieces
Your heart beating stronger still
And the lingering rose water that anointed your lover's neck
Their wrists
Will evaporate from memory
Until only the sweetness of your healing remains

I will not recycle my trauma into my personhood
I am more than mistakes men have made
And the tears I have cried
I exist on the other side of pain
Shaped by the will to survive
Survival is not enough, I want the lightness too
I want the joy, the unbridled laughter that follows youth
I am more and more again
A complex therapy of beginnings and not ends

My wealth comes from the knowledge
I have of what is 'enough'
My richness is the appreciation of what I hold in my hands
Before it slips through my fingers
I am not lost searching for tomorrows while losing todays
I am the breath from this moment
Without title on my brow
I live in the sun and its rays
Without craving for a crown
I am rich for myself, in gratitude I trust
The voice which deep inside sings, "I, too, am enough."

Equality is a veiled truth in my motherland
It is places men can go but women cannot
It is the expected silence of housewives
As they pour their husband's tea, scalding only to glasses
And never for uneven temperaments
It is telling women, myself included
That we can be anything
That the divide does not exist
That we can be free in our womanhood
Except not like that, there are always rules to abide
Written by a patriarchal scribe
Even when we split the sea into the west
And root homes in foreign soil
There is always some way to resurrect the violence
To turn fabric into a noose
To break vows written on paper by the stories
Written black and blue over a woman's skin
Calling the beginnings of decency
Feminist equality
Is a well-deployed ruse
For a society of power-hungry men
Who forget they were once women in the womb

People can love you deeply
And still not meet you where you need to be met
In your pain, in intimate understanding
Of the genesis of how you became fearful of the rain
How you wince before the thunderclaps in the sky
They cannot innately understand why you hug yourself
When the sky darkens
Why you don't answer the phone when it pours
They will not have the answers to meet you
To ease what has been hurting
Even if you have convinced yourself that the ache
Could be filled by their frame
People can love you deeply and still not tender the void
When it rains

I am grateful for each person
Who looked me in the eyes and spoke the truth
Even when my eyes were wet with tears from it
Thank you to whoever gave me what I needed
When I was determined to not want it

I steep oleander leaves in a clear jar
Seal it tight and keep it stowed under my bed
There is a comfort there, knowing it is near
The only poison being my own dread
For the tiredness I cannot sleep away
For when the gods call on me
I steep into a clear jar, oleander leaves
Floating in the water, I often take a peek
On the low days I hold the jar like a babe
And kiss it on both cheeks
There is romance in everything
I think, I know, even this
That I can distill my own poison
Give it cradle and kiss
So many poisons kill us
That are less clearly seen
Than my bottle of fermented oleander leaves

The surface is a safer place to be
But my love survives
Only in the deep

I sit outside in the summer rain
When the sun is warm against my skin
The water that pours rushes to the earth
And as quickly as it came, dissolves from its birth
That is the essence of so much of how I feel
Feelings fleeting against a seasonal wind
My tears roll back into my eyes
Almost as soon as they begin
I don't pour the way I used to
Something has blunted me from my pain
I don't pour the way I used to
I'm a vanishing summer rain

Your wounds can liberate an awakening
But beginnings can hurt
Like our first breath outside the womb
Translating air into our lungs from water
Gasping in a foreign realm outside of flesh
Outside our mother's warmth, the country of her
My rising meant meeting every toxic trait
In the face
Acknowledging the pain I have caused
The ghosts I have been
That I am as much a villain in story
As I am victim
Predator and prey
Who my mother raised me to be
And who my mother tried to protect me from
I am recovering from all the women I have been
Some more than others
Preparing myself for all the women I will become

I run into myself, the feared imposter
Draining my intuition, my creativity
Every time I challenge my worth
Decide that I have dignities to prove
But there is nowhere left to run at night
Alone in bed, with covers like a second skin
Retiring from the day into a cocoon
In my dreams I am free
I become restored by the moonlight
The dance of darkness and the celestial glows
Heals me into tomorrows
Where I answer to no demons
Not even my own

You have so much light in you
That the Sun aches
You deliver mornings to the horizon
You disappear shadows and restore the souls they envelop
You warm trees that had their leaves shaken by the cold
You are eternal greatness in glimmering gold

Weaponize my past against me
And I will serve no part in your future
You will only wound yourself
Trying to cut me with fractures
That I have already made peace with

In the presence of friends, often my darkness recedes
It creeps up sometimes, in the thick of our sniggering
They do not understand all the voids
Many they cannot fill
But they stand alongside me and listen to them still
I share with them my joy, my woe just the same
They create such comfort
That my worries disappear from frame
They do not have all the answers
And I could not want them to
It is enough that they stay by my side
As loyal as they are few

My home is not the home I grew up in
There will be no raised fists here
No shouting, no broken plates
No eggshells or shattered glass to creep over
You will not need to calculate each word
As it pours from your mouth
Scared the weight of one may tip the scales into chaos
'Caution' will not be your middle name
'Silence' will not be your first
My home is the home of love
My home is the home of comfort
My home is the home of safety
When you step past my threshold
You are welcome with open arms
Cradled with good food and tea
Lulled to sleep by prose pulled from bookshelves
Teeming with reads
When you sleep
You will rest
Without keeping one eye open for safety
Ready to spring from your bed
At the sound of raised voices
When you wake with the sun, you will be reborn again
In the comfort of knowing
You have sanctuary from the world
That you may not fit perfectly anywhere
But can find belonging here

Adjust your crown and grow your throne
You have fallen lower than here before
Each time you rise and rise again
You learn that falling is not failing and this is not the end
So, rise to your feet, as your reign demands
You have the power to shape your future
In the palm of your hands

I am a goddess of destruction and I do not lay waste to the land
I destroy versions of myself that need to be buried
A shell in the sand

I am a goddess of destruction and I lead in paths unmapped
I destroy to restore, so that what was once broken can come back
Family expectation, the skin off my back

I am a goddess of destruction and I will not be scolded into stillness
I break tradition on my knee
My queerness has saved me when it could've been a death sentence
I am unsullied
I am free

Death comes to my door at night
Bones clattering from the rain
I welcome it in and warm the kettle again
"How long has it been this time?" I ask
Although I already know
"February, it was," Death says
I remember the roads were dusted with snow
"Who is it this time? Who did you take?"
My voice breaks
Ready for tears to flow
Death only smiles and perches its boney feet on the ottoman
"No one," it says as I pass it a warm cup of Earl
"I am here for your grief. Its time has come."
It says
"I am here to dead the pain that I once brought."
The words slap me in the face and I stumble to the floor
"I don't want to forget," I say, "but I don't want the hurt anymore."
Death sips its tea, and I can almost see
Its thin, ragged skin blush warm over bone
"You will not forget your loved ones, dear,
when you stop grieving them."
Death laughs, setting its empty cup down
"But in acceptance, your grief can live alongside Life and
invite better company than what sits on your settee now."
Death says we will always remember
Even if the details slip away

I will always remember the ones I loved
Their importance will be locked in memory
How they made me feel, a fond reverie
As Death takes me by the shoulders
Places a hand above my breast
I feel the tears collect from my eyes
The tight strings loosen from my hurting chest
I feel free
A weight is pulled from me, the salt of crying endlessly
Some nights
When Death knocks at my door
It is Life in disguise

The literacy of my people that lived from the land
Is coming back to me through my grandmother's hands
I think of her now, the old frames of her life
The way she raised a town and peopled a mountainside
From one husband and wife
The herbs that they grew wild under the sun
Fed the skin and the organs, an instinctive connection
The clay from the mountains, cobbled thick skin on their feet
Soles echoing the heartbeat of the land with each step
Even in the progression of time and across seas
The body does not forget
This is not a new age, a dawning trend
This is recalling the wisdom of our ancestors' end
I know it in my bones, the shoots of a plant uprooted
The nectar of this wisdom is still as sweet now as then
It remains undiluted

Too often we are ready to speak
Without being willing to communicate
Listening to respond, to levy weapon
Delivering wounds with the violence of an angry tongue

Take a lover who makes you better
Who challenges you, whose ambition rivals your own
Who elevates your thinking
You will find endless pleasure with a lover
Who understands your dreams
Because they've dreamt them too

My people almost forgot their mother tongue
When the invaders came
When they trampled over cities
Plastered over ancient names
It wasn't the soldiers and their brawn that kept us speaking
To our olden gods
It wasn't the clang of swords
Or blood spilled from blades drawn
That kept the footnotes of our history
In speech and tongue
It was an artist, a poet, for which that bell was rung
Sometimes I doubt myself and the hands I use to create
Yet an artist's hands have shaped so many fates
Strength in beauty, divinity in song
Art can survive a nation, as it did my mother tongue

My mother taught me
That the sun shines first on those
Who choose to stand for the light

Smoke blows across the countryside
The world is all but flame
Still, a grey suit stands in front of a sea of cameras
Curating the right words, soothing burns of perception
Extinguishing outcry
For things to stay the same
Even when our Mother is dying
The one from which we all take root
The Earth gave birth to us and the soil
Her breath is the air that is thick with soot
How can industry cure what industry stole
With a fabricated lie
As if the oceans aren't drowning in fishing lines
As if the creatures aren't being dredged up by the ton
So that a corporation can levy blame on the sum
When they are the ones burning the forests
—our Mother's lungs
The clouds are heavy with ash
When it rains, the water recycled is black
The world is all but a single flame
With only one solution: land back, land back, land back

Your body deserves more
Than to be canvas to a man's rage
Hanging in doorways when you want to leave
Fists through walls to weaken your resolve
Crumpled on the floor awash in his own tears
Bitter for the salt of wounds you cannot nurse
Mother's milk soured on a lover's tongue
That paints you black and blue
And calls it love

I stumbled into womanhood without grace
I cried the first time I bled
In two ways I was rain
I did not want to bleed
I wanted to cut out my would-be womb
I wanted to resect the part of me that sounded like
The word Mother, without the M
Chalk in my mouth, spelling out a foreignness
A divorce from my body
An alienation
Packing bags with nowhere to go
How natural could this be if on instinct
It summoned the worst in me
How could I embrace womanhood
If I could not embrace this quintessential thing
This definitive rite
But some women never speak in red
Some even are caught between the biology of men
And the spirit of the feminine
So many exist in between
I stumbled into womanhood without grace
In learning that it bears different faces
Saved me, allowed me to accept that
Womanhood is not always beautiful and beloved
There are quiet moments of resentment
And I am allowing myself to exist in the space
Where I define that power in colours I choose

On the days that I want to sink into my sheets
And pour dirt over my eyelids
So that my sleep can comfort a grave
I think of the worried look on my mother's face
So, I get up, shower, wash my face
Swipe a pomegranate red over my lips
Enough colour to convince her I am alive
Put together as I should be, put together as I should feel
Such a little thing that to her says,
"I'm okay," and lets her heart beat in pace
Anything to the contrary would invite questions
"Why are you depressed?"
"Are the meds not working?"
"Have you been eating enough fruit?"
And that is all more exhausting
Than an innocent tube of lipstick
That could pull my smile over my teeth
In the shade of comfort
For my mother who loves me
But not enough to understand
That I am ill
Despite the pomegranates she has fed me

Mercy waters seeds of understanding and growth
Where vengeance summons tears that waters graves
When you speak, Time listens
It forges realities from your wordy incantation
Summoning goodness or its end
When you speak, you create the nature you will live in
A spell of intention springing to life the love you sent out
Conjuring the wickedness your spite invited
Choose your words as you choose your life
We are all but webbed things connected immaterially
To material truths that make our humanness
Such a fragile bud for bloom

I own everything that has happened to me
I own my past and my creation
I am liberated by the truth of my growth
That stands in contest with stagnation
You cannot bring shame to my house
When I've strengthened each post with the reality
Of my humanness
I am flawed, I am fractured
In these creases, God shines through

When I explored my own pleasure as a woman
It shook the foundations
Of what I'd be taught to know
About intimacy
That I've journeyed from fear of my body
To naming each part by sensation and sigh
Is a power that raised me from my knees and subservience
And drew a lover down to theirs

So many demons haunted my bloodline
Until I exorcised them from my acceptance
I am a breaker of cycles and chains
I will not become a ghost
Animated by my ancestors' dysfunction

Choose yourself and you will choose wisely
A woman is not made by how she is bent, selfless
A humble restitute for a man's ego
To be self-serving is to elevate yourself
And when I elevate myself
I elevate all who love me

Sometimes we are so seduced by the idea of survival
That we forget to create a life worth surviving for
You deserve the abundance you scraped and clawed for
Desert your hardened guise, soften your warrior stance
Allow your heart to sink back into your chest
Recede from your throat where it has been living for years
Fighting to speak your truth
You know the proverbial war
Of your four-walled home is over
But the shrapnel still sings in your skin
Bursts into moments when you finally thought
You caught up the peace of quietness
You are the lovechild of conflict and healing
Share equal parentage with the need to survive
And the need to exist outside of survival
These feelings will always mingle inside of you
Echo softly into your daily musings
But you must persist into the other side
Where the beauty of living without fear of
But appreciation of life exists

Sweat beads at my temples, rolls down my cheeks
Leaves streaks, the envy of my salt tears
I whisper as softly as a prayer
So that only God can hear me
"I am sorry," I manage to the mirror
Inspecting the mats forming in my hair
The pimples bubbling under my skin
A tender mass of scar tissue and regret stands before me
I am quick to survey every flaw
Then, a wave of guilt washes over me
The hypocrisy that I should preach lovingness to oneself
And then meet myself in the quiet moments
Without mercy, a snarl curled over my teeth
Ready to tear the last bit of confidence
From my own skin, until I am only bone
The iron of my blood collecting
To feebly shield me from this sermon of critique
Even as I stand bare, a marionette of dancing bone
I wonder why I have convinced myself
That I am unworthy of the acceptance
I had transformed into gospel
And fed into the ears of women I barely knew
"I am sorry,"
I say,
Clutching to the porcelain bathroom counter
For loving myself some days less than I would a stranger

I have an unmatched fondness for words in pen and paper
Words that would burn in my throat said aloud
In ink, my secrets live on the pages of my journal
Revelations emerge as well
Comfort, even
What I could be afraid to let hang in the air for generations
Can sit comfortably in its truth on an 8x11
Tears rippling the margins of a once taut, bound page
We all have words begging to be spilled from us
Fearful they may slip into the wrong ears
Be heard in the wrong way
But the paper is a sanctuary devoid judgement
A refuge of open arms
Waiting for you to sink into their embrace
We are all writers with stories still to tell

I want every woman I know
To experience the joy of belonging to herself

My confidence is impregnable against the world's opinions
Because I have given birth to myself
In so many phases
Delivered myself from so many heartbreaks
That nothing short of joy will be allowed to seed in my soul

My dearest pomegranate
How you began as a dream to a sapling
That could barely hold its arms up
Then grew full under its care
Taking nourishment from the Earth, the Sun, the Sky
How you ripened over time and element
How you sweetened despite
The storms you were exposed to
The jewels of wisdom and kindness
That ferment on the tip of your tongue
The worlds that live within you
You are a marvel of unspoken hopes from generations
Surviving bloodlines that succumbed to rot, to breaking
How you've endured to become
The thick skin that protects you and the ones you love
Everything that you have learned
From your inception on a wavering branch
To your maturation that shook you free
From what could no longer grow you
Tumbling into an existence wholly your own
Wherever you land, the soil rejoices
Knowing where you choose to take root
Beauty will follow

Acknowledgements

Thank you foremost to my friends and family, who
generously offered their eyes and ears throughout
the conception of this anthology. Thank you for
showering me with the love and support I needed when
I was growing from doubt. Your
kindness means everything.

Thank you to my cherished and talented friend, Cade
Cran, who created the illustrations that bound this
collection with beauty beyond what I had envisioned.
Thank you for sharing your gift so that I could
share mine.

Finally, thank you to my readers. Thank you for opening
your hearts (and your bookshelves) to my work.
Thank you for giving my words a home.

Manufactured by Amazon.ca
Bolton, ON